Who Was Here?

Discovering Wild Animal Tracks

Who Was Here?

Discovering Wild Animal Tracks

To Raul, Ruthie, Nathan, Jesse,
and Dunkin with love —M.P.

ISBN 978-0-545-93070-3

12 11 10 9 8 7 6 5 4 3 2 1   15 16 17 18 19 20/0

Printed in the U.S.A.   40

First Scholastic printing, December 2015

Main body text set in Shrub bold
Typeface provided by Chank

Who Was Here?

Discovering Wild Animal Tracks

Mia Posada

SCHOLASTIC INC.

The huge furry paws of an animal sank
into the soft mud of the riverbank.
Leaving deep footprints, with dagger-sharp claws,
the beast lumbered on, a fish snared in its jaws.

WHO WAS HERE?

A bear!

This is a black bear. Bears have five toes, just like humans, with a long claw on each toe. Bears are heavy, so their tracks are often pressed deeply into the ground. Male black bears can weigh up to 400 pounds (180 kilograms). Some are more than 6 feet (1.8 meters) tall when they stand on their hind legs. That's as tall as an adult man! They live in forests and eat mostly plants, but they also catch fish in streams and rivers.

A hunter traveling by full moon's glow
left paw tracks in fresh forest snow.
Racing through the night with its pack,
chasing its prey, teeth bared in attack.

WHO
WAS
HERE?

Nearby are the tracks of the prey that fled,
branching antlers crowning its head.
With heavy hooves pounding the ground,
it escaped into the forest with barely a sound.

A wolf

This is a gray wolf. Wolf tracks look like huge dog tracks. Wolves and dogs are members of the same animal family. Gray wolves live together in packs, or groups. They are strong long-distance runners. A pack may travel 25 miles (40 kilometers) a night to hunt animals such as deer, beaver, and rabbits.

and a moose!

Moose are the largest type of deer. Male moose may weigh more than 1,400 pounds (635 kg)! They have wide cloven, or split, hooves that help them walk in deep snow. They also use their strong hooves to defend themselves against predators. Only male moose have antlers. The moose's antlers will soon fall off for the winter, but new ones will grow in the spring.

A long-toed jumper in the arid Outback
hopped through the dry brush and left this track.
On strong legs, it bounds about,
while snug in its pouch, its baby peeks out.

A kangaroo!

This is a red kangaroo, the largest type of kangaroo. Red kangaroos grow to about 6 feet (1.8 m) tall and weigh about 200 pounds (90 kg). Their feet are long and narrow but very strong. Thanks to their powerful feet and legs, kangaroos can jump more than 25 feet (7.6 m) in one leap. They use their long tails to help them balance while jumping. They can hop as fast as 35 miles (56 km) per hour.

The African sun at bright daybreak
reveals huge footprints at the edge of a lake.
Underwater's this animal's favorite place,
where this hefty giant moves with grace.

WHO WAS HERE?

Long, narrow toes left a second track.
This animal rides on the other's back.
It munches on insects flying by
and soars into the grassland sky.

A hippo

and an egret!

Hippos have four toes on each foot. The toes have webbing between them to help them move easily in water. Hippos are huge. They can weigh as much as 8,000 pounds (3,630 kg)! But in the water, they can bounce and even float. Hippos live in central and southern Africa. They spend most of the day underwater but come out at night to feed on grass.

This bird is a cattle egret. It has four narrow, branching toes on each foot. Cattle egrets can be found all over the world. They like to live near large grazing animals like hippos, which disturb and stir up insects that egrets eat. Egrets often perch on the backs of larger animals.

A saw-toothed swimmer left this trail,
dragging its flat, paddle-shaped tail.
Its family works as a busy team,
piling sticks to build a dam in the stream.

A beaver!

Beavers have five long toes. Their hind feet are webbed to help them swim. Their long, flat tails help them paddle through the water. When they are alarmed, beavers slap the water with their tails. This loud sound warns other beavers of danger. Beavers have strong, sharp front teeth that they can use to cut down a tree in minutes. They use tree trunks, branches, and mud to build dams in rivers and also to build their lodges, or homes. Beavers eat bark, twigs, and leaves.

Round footprints left by two-toed feet
pressed into the sand in the desert heat.
This animal lives without water for days,
traveling under scorching sun rays.

WHO
WAS
HERE?

In between, a line curves through the sand.

A track with no print of foot or hand.

This creature lies buried, just out of sight.

Its fangs ready to strike a poisonous bite.

A camel and a snake!

Camels with one hump are called dromedary camels. Camels have two large toes that spread out wide to keep them from sinking into the sand. People ride camels and use them to carry supplies in the deserts of North Africa and the Middle East. Camels' large humps store fat. The fat gives them energy when they don't have food or water. This allows them to travel a long way without eating or drinking.

This snake is a horned viper. Horned vipers grow to about 2 feet (0.6 m) long. They are venomous, or poisonous. They often bury themselves in the sand to surprise their prey. They move across the sand in a sidewinding motion, leaving S-shaped lines as tracks.

Tracks on the wet rain forest floor
reveal a predator was here before.
Whiskers twitching, climbing, creeping,
silently stalking, then pouncing and leaping!

WHO
WAS HERE?

A jaguar!

Jaguar footprints look like giant cat prints. Like most members of the cat family, jaguars have sharp claws that they can retract, or pull in, when they don't need them, so their tracks do not usually show claw marks. But jaguars often scratch trees with their claws to mark their territory, a warning to other jaguars to stay away.

Be an animal track detective!

Animal tracks are most easily found in soft surfaces. So the next time rain has made the ground muddy or snow has recently fallen, see if you can find animal tracks!

There are many clues to look for:

- How many toes does the track have?
- Do they look like tracks from paws?
- Are they hooves? Cloven hooves?
- Are claws showing?
- Does it have fingers that could grasp?
- How large is the track?
- How deeply is the track set? A light animal such as a beetle leaves shallower tracks in sand than would a turtle, which is heavier.
- Is there webbing between the toes? This might indicate an animal that spends time in water.
- How far apart are the tracks? A trotting (slow-running) animal's tracks are farther apart than a walking animal's. A fast-running or hopping animal takes all four feet off the ground at one time during the movement. Its hind feet land in front of its front feet.

Draw pictures of the tracks you see. Then think of words to describe each type of track. If you can't guess what animal left a track—or think you know but want to be sure—you can look in a field guide or check one of the websites on the next page.

See if you can identify the tracks on this page.

Websites

Animal Tracks
http://www.maine.gov/sos/kids/about/tracks.htm
Find more examples of animal tracks here.

BioKIDS Tracks and Sign Guide
http://www.biokids.umich.edu/guides/tracks_and_sign/
An animal leaves behind tracks and other signs that it was nearby. Use this guide to help you figure out just what that animal was!

Further Reading

Arnosky, Jim. *Wild Tracks! A Guide to Nature's Footprints.* New York: Sterling, 2008. Check out more animal tracks in this fact-filled picture book.

Berkes, Marianne. *Over in the Forest: Come and Take a Peek.* Nevada City, CA: Dawn Publications, 2012.
Jump like a squirrel, dunk like a raccoon, and . . . uh-oh . . . watch out for the skunk! Learn the ways of forest animals, count the babies, and search for hidden animals.

Morlock, Lisa. *Track That Scat!* Ann Arbor, MI: Sleeping Bear, 2012.
When Finn and her dog Skeeter set out on a hike to cure their restless feet, they literally take a step into nature. A big, gooey step . . . right into scat (also known as poop). Scat, along with foot or paw tracks, can tell a lot about the creature that made it.

Posada, Mia. *Guess What Is Growing Inside This Egg.* Minneapolis: Millbrook Press, 2008. Animal babies are hatching all over the place. Can you figure out who's who?

Tracks clockwise from top left: duck, squirrel, raccoon, dog, beetle, cat